Highway Q & A

Joe Kells

Adam and Charles Black
London

Published by A & C Black (Publishers) Limited,
35 Bedford Row, London, WC1R 4JH

© The Estate of Joe Kells 1981, 1984, 1986

This book is copyright under the Berne Convention. All rights are reserved. Apart from any fair dealing for the purpose of private study, research, criticism or review, as permitted under the Copyright Act, 1956, no part of this publication may be reproduced, stored in a retrieval system, or transmitted in any form or by any means, electronic, electrical, chemical, mechanical, optical, photocopying, recording or otherwise, without the prior permission of the copyright owner.

ISBN 0 7136 2600 3

First published 1981
Reprinted 1982, 1984, 1986

Acknowledgements

The author and publishers extend their sincere thanks to the following for their assistance in the preparation of this work:

The Department of Transport, 17/19 Rochester Row, London SW1
The Royal Automobile Club, Pall Mall, London W1
The Automobile Association, Fanum House, Leicester Square, London WC2

The road signs from the Highway Code are reproduced by permission of the Controller of Her Majesty's Stationery Office.

Printed in Great Britain by Hollen Street Press Ltd.

Highway Code
Q & A

Introduction

Intended primarily for the novice motorist under instruction, this quiz may also be used by those who are preparing for more advanced driving tests, or who wish to refresh their knowledge of the Highway Code. The questions are based mainly on the type of verbal examination which takes place at the end of any driving test, whether elementary or advanced. One point readers should note: do not be afraid of such a test, for the examiners never try to ask 'trick' questions, or to catch you out in any way. This book should be used as an aid to your memory. It is a mistake to try to learn anything by heart. When answering questions, use your own words.

With driving lessons now costing in the region of £8–10 it will pay learners handsomely to do as much homework as possible in order to make the maximum use of roadwork practice. Hence the value of such a book as this.

Joe Kells

Questions

1 What does the Highway Code say about maintaining your vehicle in good condition?

2 In your rear-view mirror you observe a flashing green light mounted on the roof of a private car. What does it mean?

3 What is the latest ruling regarding seat belts?

4 For what types of pedestrian should you keep a particularly good look-out?

5 Explain the required procedure at a Zebra crossing.

6 Describe how you would pass animals on the road.

7 What is a Pelican crossing, and how does it work?

8 What does the Highway Code say about dogs in relation to cars?

9 What would you do if your vehicle broke down?

10 Your vehicle is fitted with a hazard warning device; what are the rules concerning its use?

11 Discuss the rules concerning parking at night.

12 Name some precautions you should take when reversing.

13 You are waiting to emerge from a side road and a lorry proceeding along the main road flashes his headlamps. What action should you take?

14 What signals are laid down for use at roundabouts?

15 What is the purpose of the areas of white diagonal stripes or chevrons painted on the road at certain places?

Notes

Questions

16 In your rear-view mirror you see a flashing blue light on the roof of a vehicle a long way astern. What does it mean, and what action should you take?

17 The reflecting studs known as 'cat's-eyes' are met with in several colours. Name them and state the purpose of each.

18 Which traffic is normally forbidden to use the right-hand lane of a three-lane carriageway on a motorway?

19 What are the main features which distinguish motorways from other roads?

20 If some object became loose and fell from your roof rack, what would you do:
   a on a normal road?   b on a motorway?

21 On a motorway, may you use the hard shoulder for overtaking? If so, when?

22 When may you overtake on the left?

23 You are the first to arrive at the scene of an accident, and there is considerable damage and injury. What should you do?

24 How long may you remain on the hard shoulder of a motorway?

25 On a three-lane dual carriageway, what is the purpose of each lane?

26 Where would you expect to see 'safety posts and discs'?

27 Which types of road do you consider to be the safest and the most dangerous? Give reasons.

28 What should you do if dazzled by oncoming headlights?

Notes

29 You are about to pass a CATTLE CROSSING sign. What specific hazards should you watch for?

30 Fixed to the lamposts at intervals along the road are small rectangular green signs with a yellow border; they carry a large white letter R. What do they mean?

31 You have just passed a sign consisting of an inverted white triangle with a red border. What does it mean?

32 Name two places where you might expect to find 'box junctions'.

33 In what respects does a trunk road differ from a motorway?

34 What is the purpose of the central lane of a three-lane single carriageway?

35 When would you not move off when the traffic lights showed green?

36 Upon which side of the road should a group of people march?

37 A continuous double white line along the middle of a road means:
   a Do not overtake.
   b Do not cross these lines.
   c Dangerous corner.
   d Overtake with great caution.
Which answer is correct?

38 What traffic must you always give way to at roundabouts?

39 You wish to stop at the side of the road; outline your procedure.

40 On traffic lights, what colour follows green?

3

Questions

41 What is a deceleration lane, and where would you find one?

42 Describe how you would behave whilst being overtaken.

43 What factors affect your stopping distance?

44 When may you use a bus lane?

45 What advice does the Highway Code give on optical equipment?

46 What is the 2-second rule?

47 In a strange town you see a white disc with a red border at the entrance to a side road. What does it mean?

48 At what distance should you, by law, be able to read a number-plate? If you could just manage to do this, would you be satisfied with your eyesight as a driver?

49 Ahead of you on a motorway is a car towing a caravan. What is his legal speed limit?

50 It has been snowing heavily during the night, and all roadside signs are covered with snow; you are on a side road approaching a major road. How can you be sure whether the sign ahead says STOP or GIVE WAY?

51 Having pulled in at the side of the road and stopped, complying with the law in all respects, what is the last thing you should do before getting out of the car?

52 Whilst you are waiting at a level crossing a train passes. The barriers remain down. How long must you wait before doing something about the situation, and what would you do?

Notes

53 It is daytime. Your car is fitted with two front and one rear fog lamps in addition to the usual quota of lights. Visibility steadily deteriorates, and you decide to switch on your lights. Which ones will you use, and why?

54 What is meant by the figure 30 in white on a blue disc?

55 You are about to stop your vehicle at the side of the road on a steep hill. Describe in full the precautions you can take in order to prevent it running away if you are going to be absent for some time.

56 Ahead of you is a white disc carrying a black diagonal bar. What is its meaning?

57 What special precautions should you take before driving on a motorway?

58 What special precautions should you take in foggy conditions?

59 What is your normal stopping distance at 70 mph?

60 Irrespective of limits, at what speed should you normally drive?

61 What must you check before driving a strange vehicle?

62 Some traffic signs are circular, some triangular and some square or rectangular. Why?

63 Having turned into a side road, you notice that at intervals there are small blue upright rectangular signs carrying a white arrow pointing upwards. Meaning?

64 Emerging from a side road onto a dual carriageway, you wish to turn right. Describe essential procedure.

65 What must you do if involved in an accident which causes damage or injury to another person, vehicle or animal?

66 You must not sound your horn:
    a When stationary, except when there is danger due to another vehicle moving.
    b Between dusk and dawn in a built-up area.
    c Between lighting-up time and sunrise.
    d Between 11.30 pm and 7 am in a built-up area.
    e Between 10 pm and 6 am in a built-up area.
Which of these is correct?

67 What does the Highway Code advise regarding alcohol and drugs?

68 Upon what occasions does the law require you to stop?

69 Where may you park on common land?

70 Ahead of you is a FORD warning sign. What must you do?

71 You wish to park on the left-hand side of the road, but see a broken yellow line parallel to the kerb. What does it mean?

72 State the meaning of the sign shown in Fig 1, page 17.

73 Describe the arm signal meaning 'I intend to turn left'.

74 Where would you be likely to see a yellow zigzag line at the edge of the road?

75 Upon which side of the road should a horse be ridden?

76 Having been stopped by the police and requested to show your documents, you find you have left your driving lieence and insurance certificate in another suit of clothes at home. What steps can you take to satisfy the law?

Notes

Notes

77 What is the correct method for negotiating a box junction?

78 You are about to turn into a side road when you see a white circular sign with a red edge; it carries the silhouette of a motorcycle above a car. What does it mean?

79 Driving along a motorway, you begin to feel drowsy. Action?

80 At dusk you see that the tail-lights of the car ahead of you have just come on. How would you know at once whether the driver is braking or has merely switched on his side and rear lights?

81 What is the meaning of the sign shown in Fig 2, page 17?

82 You have to make an emergency stop; braking causes the car to start sliding. What action would you take?

83 Having seen a ROAD WORKS AHEAD sign, you then find that all obstructions are on your side of the road. What will you do?

84 Approaching a narrow arched bridge, what common-sense precautions should you take?

85 Describe how you would approach traffic lights.

86 What is a 'filter' light?

87 Why are arrows painted on the road on the approach side of traffic lights?

88 What is the meaning of the light positioned at the side of the road in Fig 3, page 17?

89 What is meant by 'merging traffic'? Describe the relevant sign.

Questions

90 In a roundabout you miss the road you had planned to take: how can you remedy the situation?

91 Why is it necessary to have your tyres always inflated to the correct pressure?

92 You run into fog unexpectedly: what should you do?

93 Explain the difference between the signs in Fig 4, page 17.

94 What are countdown markers, and where are they used?

95 On seeing the sign for an uneven road surface what would you do?

96 Describe what action you would take if your windscreen suddenly shattered.

97 Approaching a roundabout, you use your mirror, make the appropriate signal and start to brake. The car fails to slow down. What will you do?

98 What are the meanings of the road markings in Fig 5, page 17?

99 What are the main causes of skids?

100 Name the main types of skid.

101 What action would you take in the event of a front-wheel skid?

102 How would you deal with a rear-wheel skid?

103 How could you prevent a four-wheel skid, and if one occurred how would you deal with it?

Notes

104 Approaching a road junction you see, painted on the road surface, the sign illustrated in Fig 10 on page 18. What does it mean?

105 Where would you be likely to find a single solid white line painted across the carriageway?

106 How would you adjust your driving upon seeing the sign illustrated in Fig 11 on page 18?

107 What is the meaning of double yellow lines painted alongside the kerb and parallel to it?

108 Driving along a country road, you notice that there is a centre line marking consisting of white dashes painted on the road surface. How would you know at once when there was a potential hazard of some kind ahead?

109 What is the difference in meaning between the two signs in Fig 12 on page 18?

110 Give the meanings of the three signs shown in Fig 13 on page 19.

111 Describe the sign meaning 'Wild animals'.

112 How does a cyclist or motorcyclist usually indicate that he intends to turn left?

113 Some local direction signs have a red border. What is its significance?

114 What is the overall stopping distance of a car travelling at 50 mph, and how is this total stopping distance comprised?

115 What is the meaning of the blue rectangular sign carrying a silhouette of a bicycle?

# Questions

116 Normally it is an offence to park on the 'wrong' side of the road at night, but there is one exception. What is it?

117 Describe the sign to be found on the approach to a mini-roundabout.

118 You will sometimes see a plate (Fig 16, page 19) on approaching traffic lights. Explain the meaning.

119 What do you deduce from the sign in Fig 17, page 19?

120 Say what you know about lane discipline on single carriageway roads.

121 What are the meanings of the signs in Fig 18, page 19?

122 Describe how you would leave a motorway.

123 Some level crossings have no barriers, gates, red lights or attendants. How would you negotiate these?

124 Explain the drill for a right turn.

125 At a crossroads you wish to turn right, but an oncoming vehicle signals that he intends to turn right as well. What is the correct procedure?

126 You have inadvertently got into the lane for turning left where there is a 'filter light' for traffic intending to turn left, but you wish to go straight on. What should you do?

127 Traffic at crossroads is being controlled by a police officer, and you wish to turn left. May you filter left when he holds up the rest of the traffic going in your direction on the 'straight through' route?

128 What signal would you make to the officer in Question 127?

10

129 In a narrow road (usually called a 'single track' road) which is provided with passing places at intervals, how should you use them?

130 When must you use your rear-view mirror?

131 What must you do when you stop your vehicle?

132 If you are driving a goods vehicle with a maximum laden weight (including any trailer) exceeding 7·5 tonnes, where may you NOT park it?

133 The goods vehicle ahead of you carries a sign consisting of a green diamond-shaped plate bearing the silhouette of an oxygen cylinder. Meaning?

134 You notice that at intervals along the road upon which you are driving are rectangular yellow signs bearing the letters HR in black. What do they mean?

135 What is the full information to be derived from the sign shown in Fig 19, page 19?

136 Driving in a strange town, you see first the left-hand sign of the two illustrated in Fig 20, page 19, then the right-hand one. Meanings?

137 Many authorities advocate changing your tyres around periodically in order to ensure even wear. Is this a good idea or not? Give reasons for your answer.

138 What is the meaning of the sign in Fig 21, page 19?

139 How do the two signs shown in Fig 22, page 19, differ?

140 Driving a mini car whose length is 10′ 5″, you buy some planks 14′ long and decide they will safely fit on your roof rack. What must you do when you load them?

Questions

141 What do the two signs in Fig 23, page 20, mean?

142 The figures on the sign in Fig 24, page 20, state that the headroom available is 14′ 6″, but what do the white painted dotted lines mean?

143 Give the meaning of the signs in Fig 25, page 20.

144 May you stop on the road where you see the sign in Fig 26, page 20?

145 What are the meanings of the signs in Fig 27, page 20?

146 What is the sign for a clearway?

147 At an uncontrolled Zebra crossing, who has precedence?

148 At first the signs shown in Fig 29, page 20, appear similar, but there are important differences. What do they mean?

149 How do the STOP signs illustrated in Fig 30, page 20, differ?

150 You have to leave your vehicle in a public car park. What steps can you take to ensure its safety and that of its contents?

151 What road marking goes with a GIVE WAY sign?

152 The red cover glass of one of the rear lights on the car ahead of you is broken, but the bulb is working. Is the driver breaking the law?

153 Entering a strange town, how would you know immediately if you were in a speed-restricted area?

154 Noticing that your front tyres are wearing unevenly, what action should you take?

Notes

155 What would you understand if you heard somebody mention 'wheelspin'?

156 You live in the depths of the country, and decide to fit knobbly tyres (sometimes called 'weathermaster' or 'town and country') before winter sets in. On which wheels should you fit them?

157 A driver is waiting to emerge from a side road on your left. This is the road into which you intend to turn. How can you assist him?

158 Give more than one reason for allowing adequate clearance when passing parked vehicles.

159 You run out of petrol at traffic lights where there is busy traffic. What should you do now?

160 Having accidentally run over a cat and killed it, what should you do?

161 You have to brake hard in order to avoid an accident, and the driver behind runs into the back of your car, damaging your rear bumper and his own front bumper and radiator. Who is to blame, and what should you do?

162 On the motorway you see a sign resembling a set of cricket stumps with bails over the left-hand pair of stumps and nothing over the right-hand one. What does this mean?

163 Where would it be unwise to overtake on a motorway?

164 What do you understand by the term 'long wheelbase vehicle'?

165 When driving behind such a vehicle what precautions should you particularly remember?

Notes

166 Your neighbour is teaching his son to drive and has fixed L plates to his car, which he does not bother to remove between lessons. Is he committing an offence?

167 What are the four most important things on your car?

168 When overtaking another vehicle you should, after checking for safety, pass him as quickly as possible. Why?

169 Why is so much emphasis laid upon familiarising oneself with the rules of the Highway Code?

170 Describe your behaviour at junctions and crossroads.

171 You wish to park alongside the kerb on the left-hand side of the road and notice a suitable space between cars already parked there. What is the correct drill for parking in such circumstances?

172 How are approaches to Zebra crossings marked?

173 The successful negotiation of curves at speed is dependent upon several factors. Name as many as possible.

174 What action would you take upon seeing a road sign which is obviously either misplaced or redundant?

175 Why should you avoid fast cornering in normal driving?

176 You plan to tow a caravan or boat on holiday. Need you inform your insurance company?

177 Give at least two good reasons for maintaining the correct hang-back position from the car ahead which you intend to overtake.

178 Petrol is sold in two and four star grades. What do these mean, and how would you decide which to buy?

179 Describe how you would drive in ice and snow.

180 Offer a beginner some advice on night driving.

181 You collide with an inebriated cyclist, and a passing police patrol car stops. What will the police officer require of you and the cyclist?

182 You pass a stationary bus whose driver is vigorously sounding his horn. Is he breaking the law? What would you do?

183 How does the behaviour of front-wheel-drive and rear-wheel-drive cars differ?

184 Undoubtedly you will have heard of 'double-declutching'. Why is it no longer essential for a novice driver to learn this technique?

185 Most cars in Britain have the steering wheel on the right-hand side, but some have it on the left. Say what you know about this.

186 There are two main organisations which were formed to assist motorists. What are they?

187 You wish to participate in motor sport. What documents would you require, and from where can they be obtained?

188 When applying the handbrake one should always squeeze the button on the handle. Why?

189 You have been driving an automatic car ever since you passed your test in it, and now you wish to change to a manual gear car. What action should you take regarding documents?

Questions

190 Driving entails the use of two completely separate but interdependent skills. What are they?

191 How do 'economy driving' and 'performance driving' differ?

192 How can an ageing driver compensate for his slowing reactions?

193 What is the easiest method of keeping a reasonably safe distance from the car ahead?

194 Why may it be advisable to change to the next lowest gear when about to pass the vehicle ahead on a busy road?

195 In a side road ahead you see a sports car come hurtling up to the junction with the main road, then pull up with his brakes and tyres squealing. What remarks can you offer on this?

196 You have been advised not to use too much acceleration when starting off from rest. What is the reason for this?

197 Why should you always begin braking early?

198 Skid conditions do not only occur in winter. Give one very common example of such conditions occurring unexpectedly in summer.

199 As well as dangerous conditions, there are dangerous times. Name a few.

200 What do you understand by 'aquaplaning', and how may it be avoided?

Notes

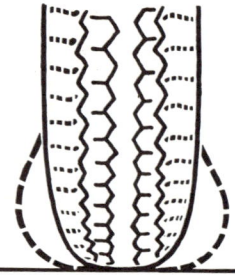 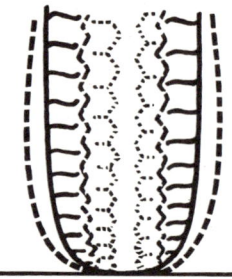 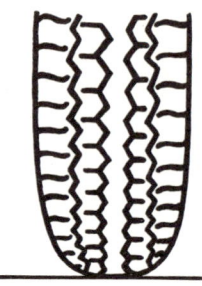

Fig 8

Under inflation causes wear at the sides of the tread.

Over inflation causes wear in the centre of the tread.

Correct inflation results in even wear across the tread.

Fig 9

'Count-down' markers at exit from motorway or primary route (each bar represents 100 yards to the exit)

'Count-down' markers approaching concealed level crossing

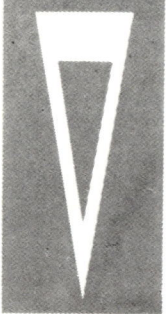   

Fig 10   Fig 11   Fig 12

18

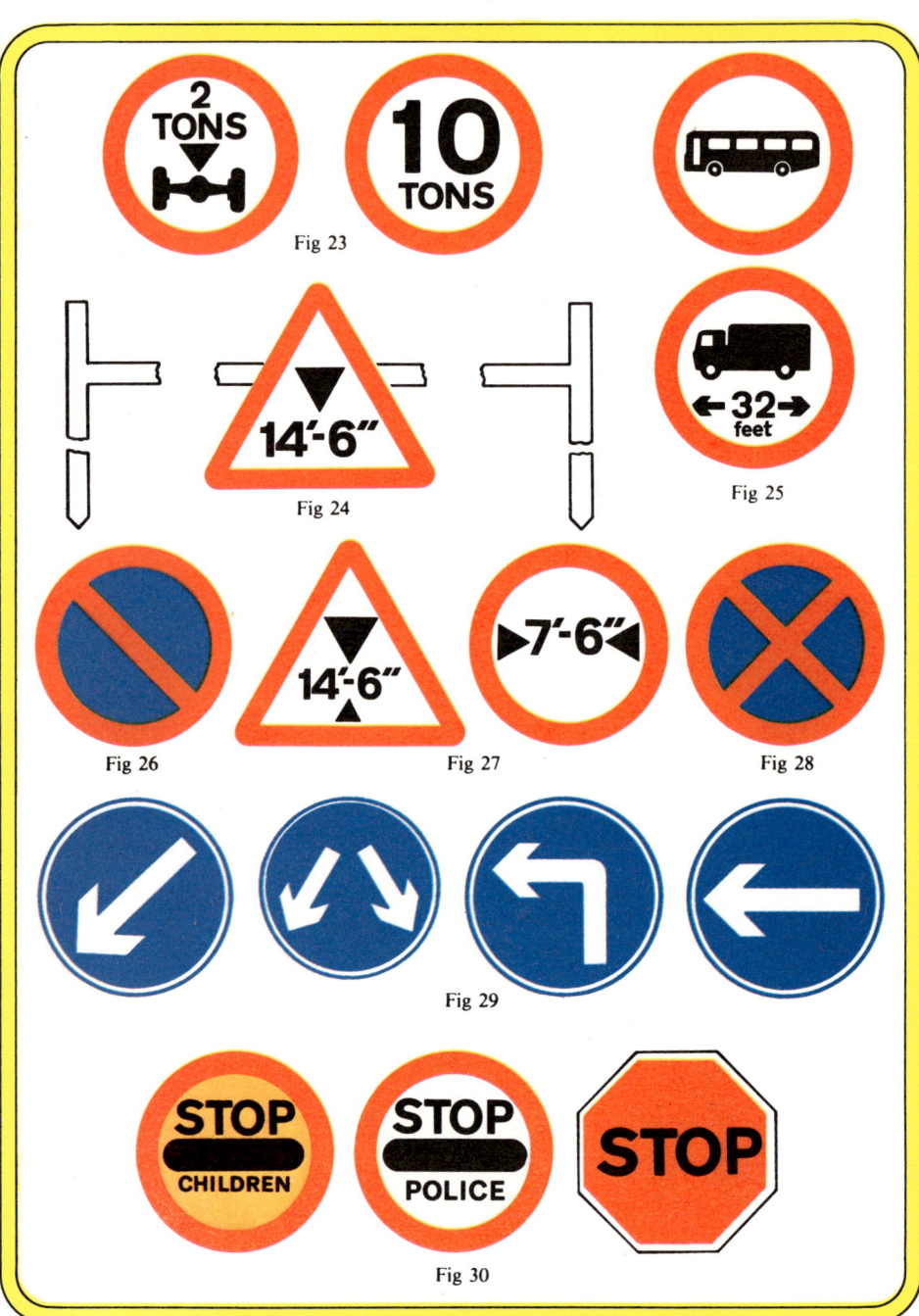

1 You are required to keep your vehicle in good condition, paying particular attention to lights, brakes, steering, tyres (do not forget the spare wheel), seat belts, demisters, wipers and washers. Keep windscreens, windows, lights, direction indicators, all reflectors and number-plates clear and clean. Should L plates be fitted, remove or cover them when the vehicle is not being used for practice or driving instruction. Do not drive with a defective or unsuitable exhaust system.

2 The flashing green light means that the vehicle behind you is being driven by a doctor on an urgent call, or perhaps by a driver transporting urgently needed blood or human tissue. In any case you should take the first opportunity to let him pass.

3 Drivers and front seat passengers in most vehicles must wear a seat belt. Exemptions include holders of a medical certificate and drivers performing a manoeuvre involving reversing, or engaged in local deliveries or collections in a vehicle made or adapted for that purpose. Children in the front must be suitably restrained, if over one and under 14 in an adult seat belt or approved child restraint, if under one year in an approved restraint suitable to their age and weight. The driver must ensure that children under 14 are suitably restrained. The safest place for young children is in the rear, wearing a properly fitted and approved child safety harness.

4 Those under about 15 or over 60 years of age. These pedestrians may be unable to estimate speed well. Watch also for blind people, who carry white sticks (the deaf have two reflectorised red bands on their sticks) or are accompanied by guide dogs. Give such people ample time to cross, and remember that they may not hear your car approaching. Watch for people getting on or off buses. Be particularly careful near schools and school crossings, where there is usually a patrol; sometimes there is an advance warning

sign in the form of a flashing amber signal. Another danger exists when you are turning at a road junction; watch for and give way to pedestrians already crossing the road at this point.

5 When approaching such a crossing keep a lookout for pedestrians waiting to cross, watching particularly for children, the elderly and people pushing prams or shopping trolleys. Be prepared to stop and let them cross. The moment they put a foot on the crossing, they are entitled to right of way: remember they are much more vulnerable than you. Signal your intention to slow and stop for the benefit of following traffic, and allow ample time for stopping on poor surfaces. Never invite pedestrians to cross, because there may be another vehicle approaching.

In the area bounded by zigzag lines you must not overtake the moving vehicle nearest the crossing, or the leading vehicle that has stopped in order to give way to pedestrians. In traffic queues crossings must be left clear for pedestrians.

Some crossings are controlled by lights, or a police officer or traffic warden; at these you should also give way to those people who are still crossing when the signal allows traffic to move.

6 Always drive slowly past animals, giving them plenty of room (horses can shy, and many animals are unpredictable). Be prepared to stop if necessary. Never sound your horn or rev your engine if it can be avoided. Remember, in country lanes, that animals could be on a lead on your side of the road; this applies in particular to left-hand bends.

7 A Pelican crossing is similar to a Zebra crossing except that it is controlled by lights which are operated by the pedestrians. The signals have the same meaning as traffic lights except that a flashing amber signal will follow the red STOP signal. When that light is flashing you must give way to any pedestrians who may be on the crossing, otherwise

22

you may proceed. Unlike a Zebra, a straight Pelican crossing with a central refuge is one single crossing.

8 When out with your dog, ensure that it is kept on a lead, and never let it out by itself.

If you take a dog in your car it must be kept strictly under control. Ensure that it cannot interfere with the driver, and never let it out of the car unless it is on a lead.

9 The first essential is to warn other traffic. If possible drive your vehicle off the road, and keep yourself and your passengers away from the road. If your vehicle is fitted with hazard warning lights, switch them on. You should carry a red reflecting triangle (on the Continent this is obligatory); place it on the road at least 50 yards (150 yards on the hard shoulder of motorways) behind your vehicle on the same side of the road. At night or in poor visibility take care not to obscure your rear lamps by standing too near them.

10 It may only be used when the vehicle is stationary in order to signify that the vehicle is causing a *temporary* obstruction to other traffic. Use it only in the event of a breakdown or whilst being loaded or unloaded. It should never be used whilst the vehicle is in motion, nor used as an excuse for stopping unnecessarily.

11 Never park on the road at night if you can avoid it. It is illegal to park at night without lights except on a road subject to a speed limit of 30 mph or less, and then only if it is a recognised parking place or the vehicle is at least 15 yards away from a junction, parallel to the kerb and facing in the direction of the traffic flow. Trailers and vehicles with projecting loads must be adequately lit.

Remember that it is very dangerous to park on the road when visibility is bad or in fog.

12 Never reverse from a side road into a main road. If visibility is impaired, get somebody to guide you. Before starting to reverse, ensure that all is clear behind, and that there are no pedestrians in a dangerous position, with special regard to children who may be in the blind spot screened by part of your vehicle.

13 According to the Highway Code, flashing headlamps have only one meaning. It is exactly the same as sounding the horn; merely an indication to other road users that you are there. In this case you should take no action.

14 If you are taking the first exit from the roundabout:
   Use the left-turn indicator on approach and until you turn.
If you are going straight on:
   Actuate your left-turn indicator whilst passing the exit before the one you intend to take. Cancel when on the new road.
If you intend to turn right:
   Actuate the right-turn indicator, and leave it in the operative condition until passing the exit before the one you actually require, then change to the left-turn indicator.
In all cases watch for correct lane discipline.

15 These painted areas are there in order to separate streams of traffic which could be a danger to each other, and also to protect traffic waiting to make a right turn. Do not encroach on these areas if you can possibly avoid doing so. Where the chevron has a solid white edge line you may cross it only in an emergency.

16 This is a public service vehicle, and belongs to the police, the fire service or the ambulance service. Keep a good lookout in your rear view mirror and permit the vehicle to pass you at the earliest safe opportunity.

17 The colours are red, white, amber and green. Their meanings are:
   Red: these mark the left-hand edge of carriageways.
   White: these mark the lanes or centre of the road.
   Amber: found at the right-hand side of dual carriageways to mark the central reservation.
   Green: these are used across laybys and side roads.

18 A goods vehicle with an operating weight of more than 7.5 tonnes, a bus longer than 12 metres or any vehicle towing a trailer.

19 They are dual carriageway roads which may not be used by: pedestrians, learner drivers, cyclists, riders of small motor cycles, slow-moving vehicles, agricultural vehicles and certain invalid carriages. There are telephones provided for use in case of breakdown, and a hard shoulder onto which you should drive your vehicle in the event of an emergency. Motorway signs, and those leading traffic towards motorways, are composed of white lettering on a blue background in order to distinguish them from others. There are no right turns, all junctions are reached by means of slip roads on the left of the carriageway. Reversing, turning in the road and driving against traffic is strictly forbidden.

20   a On a 'normal' road you should stop as soon as it is safe to do so, and retrieve the object.
   b On a motorway, use the telephone on the hard shoulder to inform the police. Never venture onto the carriageway.

21 No. Never. However, it may be used as a traffic lane when special signs indicate this, as when other lanes are closed for repair.

25

Answers

22   a   When the driver ahead of you has signalled that he intends to turn right and it is possible to overtake him on the left without either impeding other traffic or encroaching upon a bus lane whilst it is in operation.

      b   When you wish to turn left at a junction, and have checked for safety and signalled your intention.

      c   When traffic is moving slowly in queues and your lane is moving faster than the one on your right.

      d   In a one-way street, where vehicles may pass on either side, but never on dual carriageways except as in c above.

23   a   Warn other traffic by placing your red triangle (see Answer 9) or use your hazard warning indicators. Extinguish all lighted pipes and cigarettes and ask drivers to switch off engines.

      b   Inform the police and ambulance service immediately, giving the location and any other details you think will be helpful. On a motorway, if necessary drive on to the next emergency telephone.

      c   If you are sure that further injury would not result, try to get any casualties away from potential danger.

      d   Stay at the scene until the emergency services arrive.

      e   If you can, give first aid.

      f   Get uninjured people out of the vehicles and into a place of safety.

     If the accident involves a vehicle containing dangerous goods, it will carry a hazard information panel. If so, describe this to the police or Fire Brigade when reporting the accident. Keep all casual bystanders well away from such a vehicle, and even if you act to save life do so very carefully, bearing in mind that dangerous gases or liquids may be leaking. Watch also for potentially dangerous dust or vapour.

24   Remember that it is permissible to pull onto the hard shoulder only in an emergency, and that you are obliged to vacate it as soon as that emergency is over. Never forget the danger from passing traffic.

Notes

25 The left-hand lane is for normal use; the middle lane may be used when there is slower traffic in the left-hand lane; and the right-hand lane is for overtaking or right-turning traffic. If using the middle or right-hand lanes move back to the left as soon as you can without cutting in.

26 These appear mainly at the sides of winding country roads, and the discs on the posts are of two colours; red and white. They are red on the left-hand side of the road, and white on the right-hand side, to agree with the colours of the lights you would expect to see at night in traffic. They are placed there at potentially dangerous stretches of road such as where there is a ditch, soft verge or other hazard, and especially if these are at bends. Therefore a line of red lights seen ahead would indicate that you are approaching a right-hand bend.

27 The safest type of road is the motorway, or trunk road to motorway standards, which consists of a dual carriageway, each of which has more than one lane and all entries and exits only on the left. Traffic travels faster, however, so using your mirrors and concentrating are doubly important.
   The most dangerous type of road is the three-lane single carriageway, since the middle lane is used for overtaking and turning right by traffic in both directions. Before using it, therefore, be *very* sure that it is safe to do so.

28 Slow down, and be prepared to stop if necessary. Do NOT flash the oncoming driver; this is dangerous, and will merely dazzle him. Ensure that your own headlights are correctly aligned; this is the best example you can set.

29 Cattle, dogs, farm workers, etc., emerging from a possibly concealed side entrance. Also mud, manure or similar debris on the road, creating a skid risk. Proceed with caution.

30 They indicate that you are on a ring road.

31 It indicates that there is a junction ahead at which you should give way to other traffic. A plate below the sign may indicate the distance to the junction.

32 a At a level crossing.
b At a junction where two important roads cross.

33 The main differences are that:
   a A trunk road is provided with laybys, whereas a motorway is not.
   b Trunk roads do not possess the sophisticated telephone system of motorways.
   c All types of traffic are permitted on trunk roads, whereas on a motorway there are certain restrictions (see Answer 19).
   d Signs relating to trunk roads have a green background but motorway signs have a blue background.
   e There are turn-offs on both sides of the trunk road, but no right turns off motorways. Some of the more modern trunk roads have slip roads off to the left and no right turns; these are said to be built to motorway standards.
   f Trunk roads do not necessarily have a hard shoulder.
   g It is an offence to pick up or put down a passenger or hitch-hiker on a motorway, but stopping is permitted on a trunk road provided it is not controlled by the NO STOPPING sign.

34 It is intended for overtaking and turning right; but bear in mind that this lane may be used by traffic proceeding in both directions, and so be extra cautious in using it.

35 You should not move off if the way is not clear or if by doing so you would block the junction, i.e. when traffic is already waiting on the other side of the lights to proceed in the same direction as yourself.

28

36 They should keep to the left, and there should be lookouts posted at the head and rear of the column, wearing reflective clothing at night and fluorescent clothing by day. At night the leading lookout should carry a white light and the rear one a bright red light. If the column is very long, the outside rank should also carry additional lights at intervals, and should wear reflective clothing.

37 The correct answer is: *Do not cross these lines.*

38 When entering a roundabout, give way to traffic on your immediate right unless road markings indicate otherwise. Always watch for cyclists and also for long vehicles, which may have to take a different course, both on the approach and also in the roundabout.

39 First check that it is safe to do so, and that you are not likely to infringe any regulations; check your rear-view mirror, then operate the left indicator, then begin to apply brakes smoothly and bring the car to a jerk-free stop at the selected place. If there is any possibility of misunderstanding give the 'I intend to slow down or stop' arm signal before using the indicator, to give following drivers plenty of warning; merely to rely upon the brake lights is to imply 'I am stopping now', and gives no previous warning.

40 Amber. This is in turn followed by red.

41 This is a lane placed so as to enable you to lose speed when approaching a slip road leading off a motorway or trunk road. A deceleration lane is actually part of the slip road; it starts where the slip road begins, where traffic can cross the left-hand dotted line (recognisable at night by green cat's-eyes).

Notes

42 Keep well to the left and do not accelerate. Slow down if necessary to let the overtaking vehicle pass. Check your mirror to know how many vehicles are overtaking you.

43 Stopping distance is made up of Thinking distance and Braking distance. It is affected by your own speed of reaction, your car's speed and the load carried, the state of the road surface, the tyres and the brakes. It is increased by a wet or icy road, wet leaves, a loose surface or a shower of rain after a long dry spell leaving fragments of rubber and oil deposits on the road. Brake early and gently in such conditions. The shortest stopping distances in the Highway Code are for a dry road, a car in good condition and with good brakes and tyres, and an alert driver.

44 Bus lanes are shown by signs and road markings, and may operate for the full 24 hours or for other periods shown on the time plates. Details of the vehicles which may use the lanes in these periods are shown on the plates. All traffic may use bus lanes outside the specified period of operation, but never cause your vehicle to wait in a bus lane.

45 If you need spectacles in order to meet the official eyesight standard you should wear them; not to do so is an offence. Do not use tinted optical equipment of any kind (sunglasses, night driving spectacles, ski goggles, tinted helmet visors, etc.) either at night or in conditions of poor visibility. Tinted glass does not assist your vision. Spray-on or other tinting materials should never be used on windows or windscreens.

46 On the open road leave a 2-second gap between yourself and the vehicle in front, so that you can pull up safely if it suddenly slows down or stops. Two seconds is equivalent to one yard for each mph of your speed.

47 No motor traffic is normally allowed in this road between the times specified on the plate beneath the disc. The street is probably a play street.

48 75 feet for $3\frac{1}{2}$ inch letters and numerals, 67 feet for newer, smaller symbols. No.

49 50 mph.

50 If a STOP sign, it will be octagonal; if a GIVE WAY sign, triangular.

51 Having applied the handbrake, check the rear-view mirror and also look over your shoulder before attempting to open the door. Make certain your passengers do not endanger people on the footpath when they are about to open theirs.

52 Wait three minutes, then telephone the signalman from the telephone provided at the side of the track.

53 Use headlamps or front fog lamps with normal rear lights at any time when daytime visibility is seriously reduced, that is, generally, reduced to a distance of less than 100 metres. A single or two rear fog lamps may also be used in similar conditions if this helps following traffic to see you, but not simply because it is slightly dark or raining or misty. Rear fog lamps can dazzle following drivers and must be switched off as soon as visibility is no longer less than 100 metres.

54 Minimum speed limit here is 30 mph.

55 Set the handbrake. If there is a kerb, turn the wheels in towards it if facing downhill, and outwards if facing uphill, so that if the car should move it will rest against the kerb, which will act as a chock. Leave a low gear engaged; first if uphill or reverse if downhill. Ensure you have complied with Rules 115 and 116 of the Highway Code.

31

Answers

56 You have now reached the end of a restricted area, and may increase speed if it is safe to do so – up to the following limits:
Motorways: 70 mph.
Dual carriageways: 70 mph (if to motorway standards).
Other roads: 60 mph.
Note that the definition of a built-up area is where the street lamps are 200 metres apart or less. Here the 30 mph limit applies.

57 Ensure that your vehicle is fit to cruise at high speeds, that your tyre pressures are correct for motorway driving and that you have sufficient petrol, oil and water to take you at least as far as the first service area. Also check that any loads carried or towed are perfectly secure and safe.

58 Drive more slowly than usual and maintain a safe distance from the vehicle ahead of you. Do NOT rely on the rear lights of the car ahead; distance can be deceptive in fog. Watch your speed carefully, as that can also be deceptive. Remember that if you are driving a heavy vehicle it could take longer to pull up than the light car ahead. Watch for and obey all warning signals. Use headlamps or fog lamps and rear fog lamps. Ensure that your windscreen, lights, reflectors and windows are always clean. Allow more time for your journey than it would normally take, so that you will not have to rush.

59 315 ft. This is made up of 70 ft for thinking distance and 245 ft for braking distance, and assumes a dry road, a good car with good brakes and tyres and an alert driver. Stopping distances increase appreciably with wet or slippery roads, poor brakes and tyres or tired drivers.

60 At such a speed that you can stop well within the distance you can see to be clear. In other words, always drive a safe distance behind the car ahead of you, and slow down whenever bends or obstructions limit your view.

Notes

61 Make sure that it is properly licensed, and also that your own driving license is valid for the class of vehicle.

Ensure that your use of the vehicle is covered by insurance, and that there are no restrictions that will prevent you driving it.

If the vehicle is over the prescribed age, check the MoT Test Certificate – also the plating certificate (if applicable).

Satisfy yourself regarding the condition of the vehicle and any trailer it may be towing, and also the number of passengers.

Before moving out onto the road check brakes and steering and the location of all controls.

Inspect tyres to verify pressures, that tread depth is at least 1 mm, and that there are no cuts or splits.

Clean windscreen and windows and make sure wipers and washers work. Check that mirrors and number plates are clean and clear.

Test horn to see that it is working, also direction indicators.

Check all lights. The bulb(s) could have burned out, etc.

Check that speedometer works, and that silencer is efficient.

Make sure any load is secured safely and does not project.

If a car, ensure that it complies with the law relating to safety belts.

62 The circular signs give orders, those with red edges are mostly prohibitive, and blue circles with no red border are mostly compulsory. Triangular signs are warnings. Square or rectangular signs are mostly direction or information signs; those on motorways have blue backgrounds and on primary routes or trunk roads they have green backgrounds. Non-primary routes have a white background with a black border, whilst purely local directional signs have a white background and a blue border.

Answers

63 These indicate that you are in a one-way street. Such signs should not be confused with the circular blue sign carrying a white arrow pointing upwards, which means 'Ahead only'.

64 Since it is a dual carriageway, it should have an appropriate gap in the central reservation to enable you to go through onto the further carriageway, which is the one you require. If not, however, you must turn left with the traffic flow and proceed when safe to do so until you observe a suitable opening in the central reservation which will enable you to turn onto the opposite carriageway. Check mirror and signal before changing lanes in order to do this. In the gap in the central reservation wait without your vehicle protruding until it is safe to join the carriageway concerned.

65 Stop. Give your own and the vehicle owner's name and address with the vehicle's registration number, and show your insurance certificate to anyone present who has reasonable grounds for requiring them.

If you did not exchange information or show your insurance certificate at the time, report the accident to the police as soon as possible and in any case within 24 hours, either producing your insurance certificate when reporting or doing so within seven days at a police station you select (see note on page 58).

For immediate action regarding safety see paragraphs 123–127 and *First Aid on the road* in the Highway Code.

66 The correct answers are a and d.

67 You must not drive under the influence of drink or drugs or with a blood alcohol level higher than 80mg/100ml. Never drive after drinking alcohol and consult your doctor about the possible effect on your driving ability if you are taking drugs as a part of medical treatment.

Notes

68 After an accident of any kind.
 To give precedence to a pedestrian on an uncontrolled Zebra crossing, and to pedestrians on a push-button controlled crossing when the amber lights are flashing.
 When there is a red STOP light ahead.
 When required to do so by a police officer in uniform.
 When signalled to do so by a school crossing patrol.
 When signalled to do so by a person controlling traffic at a location where road works are in progress.
 At a major road junction where there is a STOP sign.
 In any other emergency after checking mirror and signalling.

69 Unless there is an official car park or picnic area, you must park only within 15 metres of a highway.

70 Upon observing the FORD sign, slow down. Try to negotiate the ford at its shallowest point in a low gear and at such a speed that no water is splashed up into the engine compartment. When clear of the water, test your brakes several times; this helps to dry them out.

71 Waiting on the carriageway or verge, except for loading or unloading or while passengers board or alight, is permitted only at the times shown on the nearby plates or on entry signs to controlled parking zones. If no specific days are indicated on the sign, then the restrictions are in force every day including Sundays and Bank Holidays. Although the broken yellow line means 'No parking during a portion of the working day' you should consult the plates for the actual permitted times.

72 This sign means 'No stopping during the times shown except for as long as necessary to set down or pick up passengers'.

73 Extend right arm straight out through car window and then move it so that the right hand travels in a large

Notes

35

Answers

Notes

counter-clockwise circle. Take care to do this as clearly as possible, so that your signal will not be mistaken for the one which means 'I intend to slow down or stop'.

74 In the vicinity of a school entrance. Such entrances must at all times be kept completely clear of stationary vehicles.

75 On the left-hand side of the road.

76 The documents required by law may be presented at a police station of your choice within the next seven days (see note on page 58). Should your car be old enough to need an MoT certificate, then this should be shown at the same time.

77 You may enter the box if you wish to turn right and the only obstructions are oncoming traffic or cars ahead of you also waiting to turn right. Never enter the box if you wish to go straight on or turn left and there is traffic blocking your exit.

78 'No motor traffic is allowed in this road'.

79 Wind down your windows to admit fresh air. Switch off radio. Pull in at the next service area and treat yourself to a cup of coffee or a cold drink, then walk around to encourage wakefulness. If you are still drowsy, at least you are now in a safe place where you can have a short nap in the car; if you feel sufficiently refreshed, proceed to the next service area, but if in the slightest doubt do NOT proceed until fully rested.

80 If he has switched on his side and rear lights his number-plate will be illuminated; if he is braking it will not. This is a fail-safe observation, for if the number-plate is not lit up you will of course automatically brake when you see his red rear lights. Should his number-plate bulb be defective, however, you have taken defensive action.

Notes

81 This sign warns that you are approaching a double bend. The bends are in the order actually shown on the sign, i.e. a left-hand bend followed by a right-hand bend.

82 This means that braking too vigorously (probably due to panic) has caused the wheels to lock. The correct action is to release the brakes and brake again more carefully.

83 The fact that the obstructions are on your side of the road means that you should give way to oncoming traffic, and proceed only when you see that the road is clear for you to pass the obstructions.

84 Position your car so that you can see if there is any oncoming traffic; if this is neither possible nor safe, use your horn to announce your approach to the bridge. Should you be driving a high-sided vehicle or towing a boat or caravan, position your vehicle so that you will be able to negotiate the bridge by passing through the centre in order to avoid fouling the sides.

85 Check your rear-view mirror and slow to such a speed that you will be able to stop at once should the lights turn against you. The reason for checking the mirror is to ensure that the driver behind you is hanging back sufficiently to be able to stop when you do.

86 A 'filter' light is one which carries a green arrow. It means that if the road is clear you may proceed in the direction of the arrow. You may go in the indicated direction whatever other lights may be showing.

87 The arrows which are painted on the road surfaces at traffic lights are so placed as to enable traffic (especially that being driven by strangers to the district) to position itself in the correct lanes ready for when the lights change. The absence of such aids would undoubtedly cause confusion. (See Fig 6, page 17.)

Answers

88 Showing red and amber, this light means STOP. Do not pass through until green shows.

89 Traffic is said to 'merge' when two traffic streams join. For instance, traffic joining a motorway uses the slip road to merge with the main stream already on the main carriageways. Similarly, one motorway or trunk road may merge with another. The relevant sign is the standard warning triangle carrying a silhouette of a side road merging with a main road; this must not be confused with the 'T junction' sign. (See Fig 7 on page 17.)

90 Having missed your road, you should continue to go round until you once more approach the exit you require. Check your mirror in good time to enable you to position your car for a left turn, and signal 'I intend to turn left' as you pass the exit before the one you will actually use.

91 First, because it is the law. Secondly, because incorrectly inflated tyres constitute a skid risk or the danger of a burst.
   Under-inflated tyres cause flexing of the side walls and overheating as well as wear on the outside of the treads. Over-inflated tyres cause heavy wear on the centre of the tread. Either causes uneven wear, which is uneconomical and rapidly makes a tyre illegal. (See Fig 8, page 18.)

92 The 'Fog Code' was introduced by John Peyton as Minister for Transport Industries. Here it is.
   1 Slow down; keep a safe distance. You should always be able to pull up within your range of vision.
   2 Don't hang onto someone else's tail lights; it gives you a false sense of security.
   3 Watch your speed; you may be going much faster than you think.
   4 Remember that if you are in a heavy vehicle you need a good deal more space in which to pull up.
   5 Warning signals are there to help and protect. Do observe them.

Notes

6 See and be seen – use headlights, fog lamps and windscreen wipers.

7 Check and clean windscreen, lights, reflectors and windows whenever you can.

8 If you MUST drive in fog, allow more time for your journey.

Remember that the most common causes of accidents in fog are driving too fast and driving too close to the vehicle in front.

93 The top sign warns that the road ahead narrows on both sides. The lower sign warns you that you are approaching the end of a dual carriageway.

94 Countdown markers are of two kinds; those used to indicate the distance to a slip road leading off the motorway or primary route (blue or green background respectively, with white bars, each of which represents 100 yards to the exit) and those used to indicate the distance to a concealed level crossing (these are white with red bars, each of which represents one third of the distance of the first warning sign from the crossing). Please see Fig 9 on page 18.

95 Slow down and proceed at such a speed that you can stop easily within the distance you can see to be clear, and also that is unlikely to cause alarm to other traffic or pedestrians.

96 Modern toughened windscreens are so treated during manufacture that in the event of a break there will be a clear zone in the driver's line of sight, in which case you can use this clear zone to enable you to drive off the road to a safe spot where you can remove or get rid of the ruined windscreen. Should your windscreen be of the older type, however, you may have to hit it with something to restore some degree of visibility; if this is not possible, drive off the road on the left-hand side after winding down the side windows to afford some visibility.

Answers

Do not panic, and use your mirror and signal your intention clearly.

Breaking the screen when moving will probably blow glass into the car as well as into the demister vents, so is to be avoided unless essential. Cover these vents when stationary and removing the glass, and try to collect and take away all the broken glass in a newspaper or other receptacle rather than leaving it at the roadside. Today laminated windscreens are widely preferred to toughened ones as they do not shatter, but only star or crack if hit by some object.

97 Use the handbrake to slow (but not violently), then change to a lower gear. As soon as possible pull in to the side of the road and stop – using the lowest gear and then the handbrake (or switching off the engine if necessary). Now try to establish the cause of brake failure or get help before venturing to proceed.

98 The left-hand marking consists of a double solid white line, and this means that traffic from either direction must not cross. The right-hand set of markings means that traffic on the side of the line which is dotted may cross provided it is safe to do so.

99 Skids have three main causes: excessive braking or acceleration, or sharp steering in relation to the condition of the road surface and the grip of the tyres. Contributory causes leading to the above could be incorrect reading of the road, emergency action necessitated by lack of concentration or failure to anticipate, driving too close or a mechanical defect such as a burst tyre.

100 There are three main types of skid:
   a The four-wheel skid – when all wheels lock and slide.
   b The front-wheel skid – when the front wheels are turned, but the car proceeds in a straight line.

Notes

c The rear-wheel skid – when the back of the car breaks away from the actual track being steered.

101 A typical example of a front-wheel skid is when steering round a bend which you have approached too fast, the car suddenly ceases to follow the bend and goes off at a tangent; in other words it follows a straight-line path and steering ceases to have effect. In such a case you should immediately ease back on the accelerator (this should be instinctive) and correct by regaining steering; straighten the wheels and then recommence steering. On no account touch the brakes, or the initial skid will become more complex with the risk of losing control.

102 Advice usually given in the case of a rear-wheel skid is 'Steer into the skid'. This may sound confusing, but it means what it says. For instance, if your car is breaking away to the left, then turn your wheels to the left for a moment before resuming course. Ease off the accelerator, on no account touch the brake and be prepared for a further rear wheel skid in the opposite direction – treated the same way – if, as is possible, you have over-corrected when turning the steering wheel. Assume a safe course gently as soon as rear wheel grip is restored.

103 Four-wheel skids are generally caused by excessive braking – more particularly in adverse conditions. For instance if you are driving too close to the vehicle in front and you see his brake lights come on; the instinctive action is to brake hard, with the result that all four wheels may lock and the car slide forward in a relatively straight line. If you are not careful a rear-end collision will result.

Prevention being much better than cure, you should hang back from the car in front a sufficient distance to be able to stop safely if he brakes. 'Pace needs space.' However, human nature being what it is, dangerous situations do occasionally develop. If you find yourself in such a situation, the best thing to do, provided there is sufficient

Answers

time, is momentarily to release the brakes and immediately brake more smoothly; this gives the wheels a chance to grip better. Alternatively, cadence braking – rhythmically applying and releasing the brakes – may be your best course.

104 It warns of the approach to a major road, where there will be a GIVE WAY sign.

105 Such a line is known as a STOP line, and means that this is the position in which the leading vehicle should wait at a Stop sign, at traffic lights or a police control.

106 Common sense dictates that you should use your horn as little as possible, and then only to avoid an accident. Also you should be prepared to meet ambulances on urgent call, and maybe distraught relatives, etc. Always approach and pass such a sign with caution.

107 No waiting on the carriageway for at least eight hours between 7am and 7pm and at additional times shown on plates affixed to standards or lampposts nearby or on entry signs to controlled parking zones. If no days are indicated on the sign, then the restrictions are in force every day including Sundays and Bank Holidays.

108 The lengthening of the centre-line dashes (hazard warning lines) indicates that there is some kind of hazard ahead.

109 The left-hand sign is a prohibitive one because it has a red edging, therefore it means that cycling is forbidden beyond this point. The right-hand sign indicates a route to be used by pedal cyclists only.

110 *Above left:* Level crossings with gates ahead.
Above right: Level crossing without barriers or gates ahead.
Below: Location of level crossing without barriers or gates.

Notes

111 This is a warning sign and is therefore triangular with a red border. It carries the silhouette of a running deer.

112 A cyclist, after checking that it is safe to make the turn, extends his left arm straight out parallel to the shoulder (see Fig 14 on page 19). Before commencing the actual turn he should replace his left hand on the handlebars. A motorcyclist may make the arm signal described or may signal by indicators.

113 Such signs indicate the direction to a Ministry of Defence establishment. (See Fig 15, page 19).

114 The overall stopping distance is 175 ft. This is assuming a driver who is fresh and mentally alert, a dry road and brakes and tyres in first class condition. Should the driver be tired, or the brakes or tyres not in tip-top condition, or the road surface affected by ice, snow, rain, wet leaves, gravel, etc., then the stopping distance will be appreciably more. Thinking distance and braking distance contribute to make up the total stopping distance, and at 50 mph these are 50 ft and 125 ft respectively.

115 It indicates a route which is recommended for pedal cyclists.

116 The exception is that you may park on the right-hand side of a one-way street.

117 It is a circular blue sign with three curved white arrows running parallel to its edge.

118 These plates are placed to indicate appropriate traffic lanes at the junction ahead. The meaning of the one illustrated is: in the left-hand lane you may NOT go straight on – only turn left. The centre lane is for going straight on, and the right-hand lane is intended for either going straight on or turning right.

Notes

43

Answers

119 It indicates the direction to Sutton Coldfield if you take the next turning to the right, which will be the A38 road, off which you will find another road leading to Tamworth, numbered A4091. The fact that the background colour of the sign is green means that the A38 is a primary route or trunk road.

120 Keep between traffic lane markings, in the left-hand lane unless you are going to turn right or pass parked or slower-moving vehicles, and return to the left lane when you have passed them. Do not move unneccessarily from lane to lane, jump the queue in traffic hold-ups, or overtake on the left unless the traffic ahead is turning right or the lane on your right is moving more slowly than your lane. When you need to change lanes, use your mirror, signal well in advance and do not cause another driver to swerve or slow down.

Where single carriageway roads have three lanes, use the centre lane only for overtaking and turning right, and remember that drivers coming towards you have an equal right to use it too. If a single carriageway road has four or more lanes do not use the lanes on the right unless signs or markings indicate that you may do so.

When approaching junctions be guided by lane markings on the road or on signs.

121 Since they are triangular signs, they warn of some kind of potential danger; that on the left indicates that there is an uneven road surface ahead, and the right-hand one warns that you are approaching a hump-backed bridge.

122 Watch for the signs indicating your turn-off, and get into the left-hand lane in good time. On reaching the countdown markers, signal (after using the mirror), and as you enter the deceleration lane begin adjusting your speed so that you can safely enter the slip road.

Notes

Adjust your speed to suit the slip road or link road. Refer to the speedometer, as your speed may be a lot higher than you imagine.

123 At such crossings there will be a GIVE WAY or a STOP sign. You must then look both ways and listen to ensure that there is no train approaching before actually crossing the lines.

124 Use the rear-view mirror and signal your intention well before arriving at the junction. As soon as it is safe to do so, with your right indicator on, take up a position just to the left of the centre line of the road and in the space marked for turning traffic if there are white diagonal stripes painted on the road surface. If possible, leave sufficient room for other vehicles to pass you on your left. When there is a safe gap between you and oncoming traffic make the turn, without cutting the corner, at the same time remembering to watch for and give way to pedestrians crossing the road into which you are turning.

125 The correct procedure in such an instance is that, unless road markings indicate otherwise or it is impractical to do so, each vehicle should pass around or behind the other one. Always check for other traffic on the carriageway you intend to cross before actually making the turn. In some cases where there is dense traffic, or where the road layout is impractical for offside-to-offside passing, it is necessary to pass nearside to nearside. Watch very carefully for oncoming traffic, which could be screened by the other vehicle.

126 In this case you should make the left turn in order not to impede other traffic. Later you can either reverse into a side road and return to the junction, or use another route to regain your original course.

127 Not until he signals you to do so.

Answers

128 You would extend your left arm with the palm of the hand to the front and parallel to the shoulder as a motorcyclist does, holding the hand close enough to the windscreen to enable the officer to see it easily, but not touching the windscreen because this could cause smears.

129 When you see a vehicle coming towards you, or the driver behind wishes to overtake, pull into the next passing place on your side and wait. If it is on the other side, stop and wait opposite the passing place. It is good manners to give way to vehicles coming uphill where possible. Never use these passing places for parking.

130 As frequently as possible, but in any case before signalling your intention to slow down or stop, or to make a turn or change lane, and before overtaking or being overtaken. Remember the golden rule: Mirror, Signal, Manoeuvre. You should always be aware of what traffic is following you and whether anyone is about to overtake.

131 Set the handbrake and stop the engine before leaving the vehicle. At night, switch off headlamps, but leave side, tail and numberplate lights on unless unlit parking is permitted where you have stopped. Look around carefully before opening any doors in order to avoid danger to other traffic or pedestrians. Take the additional precautions necessary if stopped on a hill. If leaving the vehicle, ensure that it is locked and that any valuables are out of sight.

132 As well as the usual restrictions, such a vehicle must not be parked on any verge, central reservation or pathway except in certain circumstances such as loading or unloading where this could only be done in such a position, and provided the vehicle is not left unattended.

133 The vehicle is carrying non-flammable compressed gas.

Notes

134 They indicate that you are travelling along a holiday route.

135 The green background tells you that you are on a trunk road – the A4 leading to Maidenhead. The next turning on the left will be the A331 leading to Windsor, off which there will be a secondary road leading to Datchet via the B376. The next turning on the right will be the A142 which would take you to Uxbridge and Watford. The second turning on the right is a minor road or country lane to Gerrards Cross.

136 The first sign you see means NO OVERTAKING and the second indicates that oncoming traffic has priority over traffic in your direction.

137 There are advantages and disadvantages in both methodically changing the tyres around and leaving them in position. The main advantage in leaving them *in situ* is that the tyres on the driving wheels will wear more than those on the other wheels, and so when it becomes necessary to replace them, one will have to change only two tyres at a time instead of all four. Also, tyres tend to become 'run in' for this particular position. Following changes in car design and tyre construction, recommendations differ. If there is no suitable instruction in the car's handbook, seek the tyre manufacturer's advice.

138 You have priority over oncoming traffic.

139 They are both triangular signs, and therefore warnings. The left-hand one indicates that there is two-way traffic ahead and the right-hand one that at a crossroads ahead two-way traffic crosses the one-way road along which you are driving.

47

Answers

140 Since the planks are longer than the car you are driving, they will obviously project ahead and astern, therefore you should affix a red cloth at each end of the planks; at night some form of red light at the rear would be best. This is advisable despite the fact that the law requires side and end markers only when the load overhangs the front or rear of the vehicle by more than 1.8 metres.

141 Both being circular and both indicating a weight limit, they must be obeyed. The left-hand sign states the weight limit per axle, whereas the right-hand sign shows that the total weight limit of a laden vehicle must not exceed 10 tons.

142 Such a sign is generally found on a bridge or tunnel, and the dotted lines indicate the width between which the indicated height is applicable.

143 Both being circular signs, they are prohibitive, and mean respectively:
 'No vehicles with over twelve seats, except for regular scheduled school or works buses' and, 'No vehicle or combination of vehicles over length shown'.

144 The sign actually means NO WAITING, but you may stop in order to pick up or put down passengers.

145 The left-hand sign, being triangular, is a warning sign, and indicates the height available under an obstruction ahead. The right-hand sign, being circular, is a prohibitive one because it also has a red border; it forbids the entry of traffic exceeding 7' 6" in width.

146 It is a blue circular sign with a red edge and two red lines in the form of a letter X. You are not permitted to stop on a clearway except in an emergency, and even then you should try to get clear of the carriageway if possible.

Notes

147 Pedestrians.

148 Reading from left to right, they mean respectively:-
Keep left (or pass on the left).
Pass on either side (usually found on bollards, etc.)
There is a left turn ahead which you MUST take.
Turn left.
The last sign must not be confused with the rectangular blue sign with a single arrow; this is found opposite the point where a side road leads onto a one-way street. In each of the above cases the arrows may also point to the right and reverse the meaning.

149 The two left-hand signs are portable ones, and therefore of a temporary nature, but the right-hand one, which means STOP AND GIVE WAY, is a permanent sign to be found where a minor road joins a major one.

150 When leaving your vehicle you should take the ignition key with you, put valuables in the boot and lock it, as also all car doors and windows. If you are parking at night try to leave the vehicle in a well-lit place. If there is an alarm or immobilisation device, remember to activate it. Remember also that anything on the roof rack is liable to be stolen. Always keep your vehicle log book, driving licence and insurance certificate on your person; never leave them in the vehicle.

151 There should be a double dotted white line across the carriageway, extending as far as the centre line of the minor road. Before reaching this spot there should also be an advance warning sign in the form of an elongated white triangle painted on the road surface with its apex towards you.

Notes

Answers

152 Yes, he is contravening the Lighting Regulations because no white light should be showing to the rear of any vehicle with the exception of a reversing light, and this only when actually being used as such.

153 If the lamp-posts are 200 metres apart or less, this zone is officially designated a built-up area, and the speed limit is 30 mph, unless otherwise specified by 'repeater' signs affixed to the lamp-posts.

154 The fact that only the front tyres are affected means a steering fault. Take your car to a garage, show the service manager the pattern of wear and ask him to check the tracking in accordance with the workshop manual.

155 'Wheelspin' is when one or more wheels actually rotate without contributing to the motion of the car, such as when a rear wheel spins on snow or ice (in a rear-wheel driven car). One advantage of front-wheel drive is of course the fact that the weight of the engine, gearbox and so on is immediately over the driving wheels, so affording them a better grip.

156 On a front-wheel drive vehicle, fit them on the front wheels, otherwise on the rear wheels.

157 By making an arm signal to emphasize your indicator signal meaning 'I wish to turn left' and commencing to slow down early.

158 a Someone might step out from between them.
   b One of the vehicles might have its door opened without the occupant first checking for safety.
   c One of the parked vehicles might move out without checking or signalling its intentions.

159 Pull your car out of trouble by using the starter motor with a low gear engaged. This will do neither starter motor nor

Notes

battery any good, but it will clear the crossing. When stationary, use of hazard warning lights will warn other traffic to overtake you.

160 Nothing, unless you have a tender conscience. A cat is not one of the animals you are obliged to report.

161 A driver's first duty is to avoid danger ahead of him; therefore, unless there are factors which show otherwise, the implication is that the driver behind you is responsible for the accident. He should have been far enough behind your vehicle and driving at such a speed as to be able to stop well within the distance he could see to be clear. Exchange names and addresses with the other driver, and the details of your insurers. If possible, obtain the names and addresses of any witnesses.

162 The two left-hand lanes are closed, but you may use the right-hand one.

163   a At or near an overhead bridge – owing to wind gusts.
  b At or near side or slip roads.
  c In windy conditions where there are high-sided vehicles present.
  d In conditions of poor visibility.
  e When in doubt.

164 Long commercial vehicles, particularly articulated ones. Long wheelbase vehicles should, by law, carry special signs.

165 Long wheelbase vehicles require much more space in which to execute a turn, and therefore have to swerve outwards to take a corner which cars and small vans can negotiate much more easily. One should therefore keep a careful eye on such vehicles at junctions, where their size necessitates quite a large swing at the front of vehicle, whilst its rear end tends to cut the corner.

Answers

166 It is not actually illegal but removal is advocated by the Highway Code. It is somewhat akin to 'crying wolf' too often, and tends to bring the L plates into disrepute.

167 The most important things on a car are steering, brakes, tyres and lights – in that order.

168 All the time you are actually involved in passing another vehicle you are out of your own lane, and therefore occupying more of the road than necessary. This time is called the time exposed to danger, or 'TED'.
 It should be minimised by overtaking the vehicle you wish to pass as quickly as possible; after, of course, the usual safety checks, including not cutting in.

169 The more familiar one is with the rules of the Highway Code, the fewer regulations one is likely to violate and the more likely one is to be a safe, accident-free driver.

170 On approaching a junction or crossroads, carry out the following drill:-
 a Check mirror and signal if you intend to make a turn or lane change.
 b Regulate speed so that you can stop if necessary.
 c On arriving at a crossroads or junction, look right, left and right again, or wherever other traffic could come from, and continue only if safe to do so.
 d Ensure that the correct gear is engaged to match the speed of your vehicle.

171 If one merely drives into such a space, unless one drives the front wheel over the kerb, the rear end of your car will be left protruding into the roadway and will constitute a hazard to other traffic. The correct method is to drive past the space in which you wish to park and then reverse carefully into it; this leaves your car in a suitable position to drive out when necessary (after checking for safety).

Notes

Notes

172 Zigzag lines on each side of the carriageway mark the approach to a Zebra crossing.

173 a The camber in the road.
  b The state of the road surface (i.e. wet, dry, snowy, icy, covered with fallen leaves, loose gravel, etc.)
  c The state of your tyres.
  d Your own skill and experience and correct positioning.
  e The angle of the actual curve.
  f The actual speed of your vehicle.

174 Report to the district branch of the motoring organisation to which you belong, also to the nearest police station and to the local Road Safety Officer.

175 Enthusiastic cornering means unnecessary wear on tyres and can induce skids when the weather deteriorates however slightly – even on dry roads. It is also uncomfortable for any passengers and may endanger other road users.

176 As a matter of courtesy you should inform your insurers. For the purposes of the Road Traffic Act the insurance position is similar for caravans and small trailers. These, when attached to the towing car, are identified with it, and the motorist is therefore covered against third party risks for both.
  When a boat or caravan is detached from the car it must be covered by a separate policy which normally includes loss or damage. In all cases consult your insurers.

177 a A correct hang-back position is essential to allow an adequate angle of vision: in other words, to afford you a generous view beyond the vehicle which you intend to overtake.
  b An adequate distance should be maintained behind the vehicle to be overtaken in order to ensure sufficient space for acceleration so that the TED (time exposed to danger) is minimised.

Answers

178 There are drivers who believe they should use the highest grade petrol for performance, and the lowest grade for economy. This is nonsense. There is nothing more or less powerful about various grades of petrol, and four star contains no more chemical energy than two star.

The only advantage of higher grade fuel lies in its ability to resist detonations. This is an undesirable tendency for the petrol/air mixture to fire sharply instead of smoothly. As a general rule, the higher the star grade or octane rating, the more suitable it is for an engine with high compression ratio.

A quick check that you are using a suitable grade is to accelerate hard from about 25 mph on a level road. If you hear a sharp 'pinking' noise, this can mean that a higher grade of fuel should be used. Most modern cars require four star petrol, but a few will run well on two star. Consult your car's handbook.

179 In general, when ice or snow are present, friction between tyres and road surface is at a minimum. Optimum grip for prevailing conditions may be obtained by:

a Keeping your speed well below that suitable for dry roads.

b Keeping engine revs steady and tending to use a higher gear.

c Using only gentle acceleration, steering and braking.

180 a Drive at less than your daytime speed.

b Remember – fatigue impairs vision.

c Drive at such a speed that you can stop well within the range of your headlights.

d Do not wear dark or tinted glasses; they impair night vision.

e Never look directly at other headlights; slow down or stop if dazzled.

f Dip headlights when behind other vehicles, and do not drive too close.

g Maintain battery, lights and other electrical accessories in good condition.

Notes

h Never use an inside light unless essential.

i Keep all lenses, windscreen and windows (inside and out) spotlessly clean.

The age of drivers is important where night vision is concerned. Older eyes are slower to recover from glare because the retina will adjust more slowly, so the above advice is even more important for older people.

181 As the law stands, a sober driver after a collision with an inebriated cyclist may be given a breath test on the spot. Under the Road Traffic Act a cyclist also commits an offence if riding while under the influence of drink or a drug.

182 This means that the driver is summoning assistance for his crew. He is not breaking the law. You should report the matter to the nearest police station. Ring 999 if necessary.

183 The main theoretical difference between FWD and RWD cars is that they behave differently in corners. FWD drive cars tend to 'understeer' under power on a bend, which means that the steering wheel has to be turned rather more than seems appropriate; while theoretically RWD cars under power on a bend would tend to 'oversteer'. In practice, most modern cars whether FWD or RWD are designed with a mild tendency to 'understeer', a good characteristic for straight line stability and safer cornering.

184 Double-declutching is no longer an essential technique for novice drivers to acquire because manufacturers now incorporate synchromesh on all gears with the exception of reverse.

185 RHD and LHD are designed to be compatible with the 'Keep left' or 'Keep right' rules of different countries. Today a LHD car in Britain has either been imported or belongs to a visitor from a country which drives on the right of the road.

Answers

186 In Britain the Automobile Club was founded in 1897 and granted the prefix 'Royal' by His Majesty King Edward VII in 1907. It is now the British governing body of motor sport, and the F I A's representative in Britain.

The second organisation is the Automobile Association, whose headquarters are in Basingstoke. This organisation was founded on June 29th 1905.

187 The following documents are necessary:
   a Competition licence.
   b Medical certificate.

These may be obtained from RAC Motor Sport Limited, 31 Belgrave Square, London SW1.

You should also be in possession of the current RAC Motor Sport Year Book and Fixture list.

188 The reason for squeezing the button on the handbrake is to minimise wear on the ratchet. If this is neglected and excessive wear takes place the handbrake could slip whilst parked on a hill.

189 Having passed your test in a car with an automatic gearbox, you must take a fresh test before being qualified to drive with a manual gearbox. You should also inform your insurers when changing cars.

190 The two separate skills are roadcraft and control skill. Roadcraft is acquired mainly by observation, knowledge and intelligent application, whereas control skill is a matter of continual practice in the use of all car controls.

191 Economy driving entails a high degree of 'car sympathy', by which is meant gentle acceleration when cornering, gear changing and so forth. Performance driving is normally a competition technique and involves getting the most from your car's engine and handling capabilities.

Notes

192 An older driver's reactions are slower than those of a younger person in direct proportion to the difference in ages. He should therefore compensate:
    a by an increase in hang-back position, and
    b by remembering that his night vision is no longer what it used to be.

193 There are two easy methods:
    a Estimate the distance in bus lengths. (A bus length is approximately 10 metres.) Allow one bus length for every 10 mph of your road speed.
    b The Two Second rule. Note visually when the vehicle ahead of you passes a certain mark on the road or at the roadside; your distance behind that vehicle should be such that you will pass the same mark not less than 2 seconds later, irrespective of speed.

194 It is advisable to change down before passing another vehicle if by doing so you produce greater acceleration and so reduce the 'TED' (time exposed to danger).

195 Besides causing excessive wear on his own brakes, tyres and suspension, the sports car driver has also caused a certain amount of apprehension in the minds of other drivers, and this fact alone could cause an accident in which he would not be directly involved.

196 Excessive acceleration when starting from rest incurs heavy wear on the clutch plate, transmission, tyres and suspension; hence unnecessary expense.

197 Early braking means gentle braking and consequently less wear on brakes, tyres, suspension and steering. It also means you will be at a much more manageable speed when approaching a hazard.

198 An example of skid conditions occurring in summer is when a shower of rain follows a long dry spell. This results in the

Answers

road surface becoming a gooey mixture of rubber shreds, oil splashes and water, which could be absolutely lethal to a driver who is unaware of the changed conditions.

199 Dangerous times (as opposed to conditions) are:
   a Rush hours.
   b Public Houses closing times.
   c Times at which schoolchildren are on their way to and from school.
   d Scheduled times for major sporting events.

200 Aquaplaning is the effect which results from driving too fast on a very wet surface. It occurs when tyres in less than perfect condition begin to lose their direct grip on the road surface and ride on the surface of the water in the same manner as water skis. The condition may be recognised by a loss of steering response. In such a case, reduce speed by deceleration and on no account touch the brakes or a complex skid will result.

A very approximate estimation of the speed at which aquaplaning may occur is to multiply the square root of your tyre pressure by nine.

Example: Tyre pressure 25 lb per sq inch – the square root of 25 is 5 – hence 5 × 9 = 45. Therefore aquaplaning could be expected to commence at around 45 mph.

After several years the Highway Code is usually revised and issued with a new cover. In between revisions it is occasionally re-printed with the same cover, but with amendments, and dated inside the back page. The Highway Code in a driver's possession should be the latest print of the current revision.

Answers 65 and 76 relate to the Road Traffic (Production of Documents) Act 1985 but, at the time of this book going to press, the change from 5 to 7 days is not recorded in the current edition of the Highway Code.

Notes